ebay : Make Money on eBay Selling Products.. Not Excuses

How to Sell on ebay : ebay Millionaires Bible

By Marketing Guru

Published by:

Marketing Guru

©Copyright 2015 – Marketing Guru

ISBN-13: 978-1507706664
ISBN-10: 1507706669

ALL RIGHTS RESERVED. No part of this publication may be reproduced or transmitted in any form whatsoever, electronic, or mechanical, including photocopying, recording, or by any informational storage or retrieval system without express written, dated and signed permission from the author.

Table of Contents

Chapter 1:   Why E-bay?..1
Chapter 2:   Opening an EBay account................3
Step 1: Click "register" on eBay's front page..................3
Step 2: Tell eBay about yourself......................................3
Step 3: Choose a user ID, password, and security questions..4
Step 4: Prove you're a human and agree to terms 6
Step 5: Carefully check your email box for confirmation 6

Chapter 3:   How to sell on eBay - Small Business Primer for Getting Online Sales started fast with eBay..8
Writing a listing 9
Take your time 10
Make it easy 10
The anatomy of a listing 10
Category 11
Title 12
Description 12
Photographs 13
Pricing 14
Shipping 14
Listing your item 15
Keys to remember 15
EBay and PayPal fees 16

Chapter 4:   14 ways to reduce your EBay and PayPal fees 18
1. PayPal Merchant Discount 19

2. Relisting Credits 20
3. Reclaiming Non Paying Bidder Fees 20
4. Host Your Own Photos 21
5. Tweak your Starting Prices 21
6. Pay for Your eBay Fees Using a Cash Back Credit Card 22
7. Teach Yourself HTML..22
8. Open an Ecommerce Store 23
Savings Fees on Listings 23
9. eBay Shop Listings 24
10. Sell More Expensive Items.................................24
11. Reassess Your Use of Listing Upgrades 24
12. Second Chance Offers 25
13. Lower Your Starting Prices 25
14. Dutch Auctions 26

Chapter 5: Search Engine Optimization for eBay Shops 27
How Search Engines Works....................................28

Chapter 6: Why Ebay auction fails?................34
Price 35
Photograph 35
Reserve Price 36
The Listing...36
Negative feedback 36
PayPal 37
Being Difficult 37

Chapter 7: Some Auction Tips..!!.....................38
Chapter 8: 12 Items You CAN'T Sell On EBay 44

Chapter 1:
Why E-bay?

It's rare to find individuals in the United States who haven't used eBay as yet. It's almost like a million dollar industry where buying and selling is a regular act. While there are many other auctions sites that exist today, very few have been able to make a name of themselves. Most of the us are not aware about the existence of the auction sites which have been in business since several years. Primarily because these sites have not been able to make a name for themselves. Have you ever wondered why eBay is preferred over other auction sites? There are many reasons why eBay has its dominance over other similar sites. Let me unleash some reasons for you.

Reputation: eBay is almost like a brand in itself. It's been in business since several years, and undoubtedly it's a name you can trust upon.

Security Features: eBay has 128 bits encrypted security system which makes it safe to enter any of your personal information on the site without worrying that your information will be stolen.

PayPal: eBay owns PayPal so it becomes easier for you to do financial transactions on eBay as they are able to track information easily.

Customer Service: eBay offers 2 types of customer service contact. One can reach them via email or via chat. Chat service i available 24/7 and in most cases you will get immediate resolution to your problem. I have contacted eBay chat service several times, and I have been extremely happy with their service. Quick response and customer attention is the trademark of their customer service offer.

User friendly: eBay is very user friendly site. If you are already using the site, then you may know how effortless it is to enter into a deal and safely complete the transaction. There are many other reasons why people prefer eBay. I just thought of highlighting few prime reasons.

Chapter 2:
Opening an EBay account

Step 1: Click "register" on eBay's front page

Near the upper-left of eBay's front page, you should see a message that says "Welcome! Sign in or register." Click on the word "register" to begin the registration process

Step 2: Tell eBay about yourself

After clicking on the "register" link in Step 1, eBay asks you to complete a web form. This form asks for various kinds of personal information, providing eBay with enough information to open a trading account for you. In

the first area, labeled "Tell us about yourself," enter the following:
- Your first and last names where requested.
- Your street address, city, state or province, zip or postal code, and country in each labeled space.
- The telephone number you use most, along with an extension (leave it blank if you don't have one)
- Your email address. Enter it twice, once in the upper box and once in the lower box. Be sure that you enter it in the same way each time. eBay asks twice to be sure that you've typed it correctly each time.

Step 3: Choose a user ID, password, and security questions

In the next area of the form, eBay asks you to choose and enter a nickname by which you'll be known on eBay, a password to protect your account, a security question to protect your password in case you forget it, and your date of birth, which eBay must have for legal reasons. Complete this part of the form by entering or selecting a:

Nickname of your choice. After entering the name Click on the "Check your user ID" box (marked B) after you enter your nickname of choice and eBay will tell you whether or not someone else is already using the name you've selected.

Password of your choice. Each time you log into eBay, you'll be asked to provide this password so that nobody else can buy or sell in your name. Enter the password twice, once in the upper box and once in the lower box. Once again, be sure that you enter it in the same way each time.

Secret question to protect your password .Click on the list to see a series of personal questions and choose one that you can answer easily and quickly. If you ever lose your password, eBay will ask you this question in order to verify your identity before helping you to choose a new password.

Correct answer to the question that you've just chosen. Again, if you ever lose your password, eBay will ask you the question you've chosen above. The answer you provide at that time will be compared to the answer you supply here. This is a simple way for eBay to check your identity before helping you with password problems.

Date of birth. Select the month and day that you were born from the drop-down lists, then entering the year in which you were born into the box at the lower-right.

Step 4: Prove you're a human and agree to terms

Read to the best of your ability the messy, squiggly text that eBay provides.
Do your best to enter the identical text into the comparison box. If you get the text wrong, eBay will ask you to try again in a few moments. This test (reading convoluted text and then entering it) is designed to be an impossible task for "bots" to complete. Unfortunately, it is also difficult for many humans to complete, so it may take you several tries to get it right.
Read the eBay user agreement and privacy policy (click on the links marked "user agreement" and "privacy policy" in each case), then check the box indicating that you agree with these terms.
When you're done, click the "Register" button to complete the first form required for eBay registration.

Step 5: Carefully check your email box for confirmation

Once you've successfully submitted the first registration form, check your email box for a message from eBay with the subject "Complete your eBay Registration--last step." Once the message arrives, open the message and look for a button marked "Activate Now."

Chapter 3:
How to sell on eBay - Small Business Primer for Getting Online Sales started fast with eBay

To sell successfully on eBay... any business or person should establish themselves as a trusted merchant. Once an image of trust is formed you can use your eBay listings as a tool to promote your business and your products at the same time to the entire world at a very low cost. Graphics and content usually command the buyers' attention online. But as in any business, everything starts with customer service. All the pretty graphics and fancy descriptions in the world will not maintain and grow your business if your do not follow the rules and deliver the products. If you and/or your business do not know the basics of eBay selling, it will be very difficult to maintain an image of an established and reputable online merchant. Learning the basics is where everything starts in this world. Online or not, you must know the ropes to succeed.

eBay is an unmatched resource for any business in many ways beyond simply selling product. It all must start with the simple act of selling one item however –
Let's get started!

Writing a listing

Writing and eBay description can be as simple or as difficult as you want to make it. Always try to keep in mind that you are providing a description of your product for a BUYER. Write about the benefits of your product not just the specifications. Sell the sizzle and be honest. Buyers respond to honesty, especially with used items. Show the flaws, tell the honest and forthright truth about your merchandise. Writing an eBay listing doesn't always look straightforward to beginners. Keeping a few simple rules in mind will help.

Take your time

Set aside an hour to get the listing right. You'll get quicker with experience. Once you launch a listing it could get a bid right away, when a listing has a bid eBay will not allow any revisions to the original text. Spell check and get it right from the start!

Make it easy

List a product you are familiar with. If you carry a particular best seller in your retail store or business, list that item first. Think Keywords! Buyers find your listing from the title you place online. Proper Keywords increase sales!

The anatomy of a listing

An eBay listing requires information about the item, you enter this information into the "Sell your item" form

Using the eBay "sell your item" form will introduce you to all of the necessary steps required to list a single item on eBay. When you have mastered this method of getting product online via eBay you may be interested in third party applications which make this process much easier and repeatable. For now, lets look at the basics.

eBay helps you build your listing or auction for you step by step, from assigning categories to setting the price. Click on "Sell" to get the "Sell your item" form.

Category

You need to list your item in one of the 13,000 categories of goods listed on eBay, from musical instruments to concert tickets. Choosing the right category helps buyers find you. It can be difficult to choose the best categories for some items, but eBay's category selector in the "Sell your item" form can help. You can list your item in two categories if you like, but the cost of listing the item you wish to sell will double.

Title

Give your item a winning title to help buyers searching eBay find you. Cram your title full of descriptive keywords that people will be looking for. Include the name brand of the item, the color, and size if any. You should also take a look at similar items selling on eBay to get an idea about what keyword terms other more experienced sellers are using successfully to sell similar items. Later you will look at signing up for free and paid research tools like Terapeak or Hammertap to help with this research. You have 55 characters to fill up with words that buyers search for. Don't rely on guesswork - use Pulse (www.ebay.co.uk/pulse) to get the inside scoop on what buyers are searching for.

Description

Provide a written description of what you're selling. Describe your item as if you don't have a photograph. Write your blurb in a text editor and then copy and paste the text into the "Sell your item" form (after removing all formatting). Be honest and exhaustive. Include the good, the bad and the ugly: if the item is damaged, say so. Read the eBay rules regarding keyword spam. EBay forms on using tricks such as using the phrase "like Prada" or "Similar to Rolex" when your item is not a Prada or Rolex branded piece of merchandise. Just stick with the facts but do it will style and use the benefits of your items to sell the buyer on why they want to purchase from you!

Photographs

Proper photos are essential to stellar sales, so make them clear and crisp. Try to use natural lighting rather than the small flash on your point and shoot digital camera. Keep the background solid and only have one subject in your photograph. Using scantily clad models may sell product but be careful of your image. When selling something of high value include more than one image, at multiple angles, and progress around your item with the images to give a complete picture of what it is your selling. Pictures sell and video is even better.

Pricing

Protect yourself by starting your auction at the lowest possible price you're willing to accept. Remember that lower start prices do attract more bids, earlier in the auction. If you have some good feedback and have created a good listing, think about starting your auction off at .99 cents. Starting this low will attract interest and, bids - the more bids the more traffic to your listing. Traffic to your listing increases bids, get the picture? eBay is a marketplace which establishes true market value of merchandise. If you place your product correctly, the market will respond favorably.

Shipping

Using the included eBay shipping calculator is essential to sales. People are very aware of the shipping scams other sellers have been using for years on eBay. (You know the story: $25 >1lb item listed for .99 cents on eBay with flat rate shipping rate of $24.99...). To sell any item your shipping costs must be competitive. If you have an established account with UPS or Fedex you should consider including free shipping for a Buy it now price. Buyers love free shipping!

Listing your item

Once you have put together all of the parts of a listing and assembled them in your sell your item form on eBay you will have a better idea of how the whole process works for the next item you plan to list.

Keys to remember

Check spelling across the board in every field.

Make sure you have accurate shipping information entered: Size of the box, weight, your zip, etc. Getting tagged for oversized shipping or shipping an item for less than you programmed into the shipping calculator can be painful lessons.

Re-check the category eBay assigned to your item: some categories sell better than others Remove any "Don't Buy From Me" text from your description: (i.e. Don't bidif your feedback is low or Don't bid if you do not plan to pay)

Keep your text easy to read with just one font selection in a limited amount of colors. Think about reading a book instead of a circus wagon.

It's fairly simple and you'll be guided through each step. Relax. You can amend and revise your description and details as many times as you like before submitting it to the site. You don't pay a fee until you list your item but also remember that once an item is listed, you do not have any way to get those listing fees back if you need to make a change which requires canceling a listing. So check your work.

EBay and PayPal fees

EBay charges you a small fee to list your item, and you'll have to pay a Final Value Fee if it sells. Listings fees range from 11 cents to $300.00 depending on the starting price and what category you list in ($300.00 if the listing fee for a 90 day Real Estate Classified listing). Final Value Fees are calculated as a percentage of the sale price. All of EBay's fees for listing and final value can be found here.

http://pages.ebay.com/help/sell/fees.html

Chapter 4:
14 ways to reduce your EBay and PayPal fees

One of the top complaints against eBay is the level of fees. It is therefore surprising that many large eBay sellers make unnecessary and easily avoidable payments to EBay Strategies for all eBay Sellers. These fee-saving strategies can be implemented by all eBay sellers, no matter what items they sell or their listing strategy.

1. PayPal Merchant Discount

If you are a volume seller on eBay, then you are probably eligible for a merchant discount on PayPal fees. The merchant fee structure is as follows:

Monthly sales volume	Website, invoice and email payments	eBay payments
Up to $3,000.00 USD	4.4% + $0.30 USD	3.9% + $0.30 USD
$3,000.01 USD - $10,000.00 USD	3.9% + $0.30 USD	3.4% + $0.30 USD
$10,000.01 USD - $100,000.00 USD	3.7% + $0.30 USD	3.2% + $0.30 USD
Above $100,000.00 USD	3.4% + $0.30 USD	2.9% + $0.30 USD

To receive discounted fees you must log onto your PayPal account and apply. This can be done from PayPal's fees page.

Potential saving - up to 2% (1% on PayPal.com) on all PayPal transactions.

2. Relisting Credits

Insertion Fees are generally non-refundable. However, eBay will automatically credit the Insertion Fee for an unsuccessful auction if:

You relist the item by clicking the "relist your item" button on the item page for the ended listing (or any other relist feature on the website) and the relisted item is sold the first time you relist it.

Potential saving: Up to £2 ($4.80 on eBay.com) per relisted item.

3. Reclaiming Non Paying Bidder Fees

If a buyer does not pay for their item, you can claim back the eBay fees via eBay's unpaid item process. An unpaid item can be reported up to 45 days after an item closes.

See http://pages.ebay.com/help/tp/unpaid-item-process.html for more details.

Potential saving: Listing and final value fees on unpaid items.

4. Host Your Own Photos

If you need to use more than one photo to describe your item, eBay will charge per additional picture. However, it is simple to host your own photos, and avoid this extra cost.

If you have an eBay shop, eBay provides 1MB of free picture storage. In addition, there are many free photo hosting services such as http://www.theimagehosting.com or http://www.pictiger.com/

Potential saving: £0.12 ($0.15 on eBay.com) per additional picture.

5. Tweak your Starting Prices

Be careful when you choose your starting price, as a very small difference in price can lead to a large increase in insertion fee, especially if you are selling multiple items. For example, an item with a starting price of £29.99 incurs an insertion fee of £0.75, whereas a starting price of £30 would cost £1.50.

On eBay.com a staring price of $49.99 incurs a fee of $1.20 where as a starting price of $50.00 would cost $2.40.

Potential saving: Up to £0.75 ($1.20 on eBay.com) per listing.

6. Pay for Your eBay Fees Using a Cash Back Credit Card

Several credit cards give cash back on money spent. By using an American express credit card to pay your eBay fees, you can receive a small rebate for your eBay fees. Bear in mind that this only works if you pay your credit card bill in full each month.

Potential saving: Up to 1.5% cash back on eBay fees.

7. Teach Yourself HTML

Many sellers use eBay's listing designer service to improve the look of their listing. If you are listing multiple items, this cost will soon add up. By learning some simple HTML or employing a designer, you can develop your own template and save on the extra listing fee.

Potential saving: £0.07 ($0.10 on eBay.com) per listing.

8. Open an Ecommerce Store

Potentially the best strategy of all is to expand your business beyond eBay. By setting up your own ecommerce store you can upsell to customers you have acquired through eBay, and pay no fees at all. Channel Management software such as eSellerPro, Marketworks and ChannelAdvisor enable eBay sellers to run an ecommerce store off the same inventory as their eBay sales.

Potential saving: You pay no eBay fees on items sold off eBay!

Savings Fees on Listings

The following fee-saving tactics involve changes to your eBay listing strategy and should therefore be considered in the light of your business objectives. For each of these tactics, run a limited trial and compare the conversion rates (% of listings that sell), average sales price (sales total/number of items that sold), take rate (% of sales that eBay takes as fees) and margin against your current listing strategy.

9. eBay Shop Listings

Despite the recent rise in shop listing fees, eBay shop fees are still on the whole cheaper than core listings. The best use of shop listings is for upselling commodity items and for unusual items that require a longer listing period.

10. Sell More Expensive Items

eBay has a sliding scale of fees, taking a higher percentage of the sale price (take rate) of less expensive items. By selling more expensive items you can reduce your take rate. For example, the take rate of a £5 item is 9.25%, whilst for £200 item it is 4.55%.

11. Reassess Your Use of Listing Upgrades

Listing upgrades are expensive, and should not be used unless they are improving sell-through rates and average selling prices. eBay research products like eSellerStreet (http://www.esellerstreet.com), Hammertap (http://www.hammertap.com) and

Terapeak (http://www.terapeak.com/) will allow you to investigate the effectiveness of listing upgrades for products in your categories. You should also conduct your own trials.

12. Second Chance Offers

eBay's Second Chance Offer feature allows more than one item to be sold from a single listing, saving on the listing fee for each additional sale. When using second chance offers, you should be aware that you are making a trade-off between price and sales volume, as second chance offers are inevitably lower than the item's final price.
Potential saving: Up to £2 ($4.80 on eBay.com) per sale.

13. Lower Your Starting Prices

eBay's insertion fees are linked to the starting price of an auction, by lowering your starting price you will encourage bidding and lower your listing fees.
Potential saving: up to £1.85 ($4.60 on eBay.com) per listing.

14. Dutch Auctions

Dutch auctions, like the Second Chance Offer, allow you to sell multiple items off a single listing, saving on multiple listing fees.

Potential saving: Up to £2 ($4.80 on eBay.com) per item.

Chapter 5: Search Engine Optimization for eBay Shops

Despite 50 percent of online purchases being researched via a search engine, most eBay sellers ignore the potential of search engines to drive traffic to their listings. By optimizing your eBay Store, your products could improve their rankings in the search results on major search engines and boost your sales.

High rankings can drive huge amounts of traffic to your products, and even with limited resources, it is still possible to apply techniques that will increase the rankings of your eBay Store and listings.

How Search Engines Works

When looking for a product, a customer visits a search engine and enters a search term or keyword, for which the search engine produces a list of results that it considers most relevant. It is by understanding how this list of results is produced that your eBay page can be optimized. The ranking of a web page for a keyword depends on three things:

The position and frequency of the keyword on the web page: When producing results for a search term, search engines will rank your pages based on the keywords they contain and their prominence on the page.

The content of the page's HTML tags: The search engine also looks at the content of the title and meta tags of the page's HTML code. Humans don't read "meta tags" - they are included on a web page to help search engines understand what the page is about, so having good meta tags that describe your website pages is important

The links going to that web page: Search engines consider an inbound link as a vote of popularity. Google, for example, gives each web page a score of 1 to 10 (called a PageRank) depending on the number and origin of inbound links. For a given search, the page with the higher PageRank will appear higher in the list of search results. When listing on eBay you have direct control over the content - and hence the keywords - you include. However, you can only access the page meta tags indirectly, through configuring your Store and listings.

Step 1: Choose Your Keywords

The first stage of search engine optimization is to choose effective keywords. To select keywords, put yourself in the shoes of your customers and consider what keywords you would enter if you were looking for your products online.

EBay Store traffic reports are useful as they contain the search terms that users are entering in order to find your listings. For example a PDA seller might choose Palm, Handheld and PDA as keywords for their Store. For the listings they also use the keywords referring to the item model number and features.

Step 2: Optimize Your eBay Presence

Repeating a keyword in a number of different places such as your Store URL, title and item description will increase the search engine's perception of how relevant your web page is to a particular keyword. However, be careful not to go overboard - "keyword spamming" is penalized by the search engines. Your description should also be clear and readable.

Choose Your eBay Store Name

Your Store name appears in your eBay Store's URL and ideally it should contain your most important keywords. For example, a bike Store seller might choose "Mountain-Bikes-UK," which would give a Store the URL http://stores.ebay.co.uk/mountain-bikes-uk

Optimize All Store Pages

The title you give your product is very important, as it also appears in the "title" tag of the listing web page, so you should include your search engine keywords.

Your product descriptions should also include your keywords. Search engines attach the most importance to words in titles and bolded words, so ensure that you have placed you keywords prominently. You should also create custom pages for your eBay Store. Custom pages are a set of unique pages you can create or edit for your Store to help showcase items and special promotions, describe the history of your business, etc. (http://pages.ebay.com/help/stores/contextual/managing-custom-pages.html).

Be sure and include effective keywords on your custom pages too.

Optimize Your eBay ID

eBay includes your User ID in the "title" tag of your About Me page and feedback pages. Your eBay User ID should reflect something about the product you sell, preferably including your most important keyword. Try and choose a memorable and individual eBay ID, as this will help customers find your eBay presence by searching. For example an eBay name like "PDA-Wonderland" will be easier to find in Google than "Online-Deals."

Optimize Your eBay Store Keywords

In the "Manage my Store" area, eBay enables the selection of search engine keywords. These keywords appear in the "title" tag for your Store pages, and so it is important that you specify relevant keywords for each page. Also make sure to include your keywords in your Store's description, as this appears in the description meta tag of your eBay Store pages.

Reviews and Guides

EBay Reviews and Guides (http://reviews.ebay.com) are a great way of driving traffic to your listings, from both inside and outside eBay. Articles you write for eBay's Reviews and Guides containing your chosen keywords and linked to your eBay Store have the potential to drive traffic to your listings.

Use Search Tags on Your Content Pages

EBay recommends using "search tags" in your content pages, such as eBay My World, Blogs and Reviews & Guides. Search tags identify topics and concepts in your content. "So if you wrote about Pez dispensers in your blog, you could use tags like "Pez," "dispensers" and "collectibles" to increase your visibility in search results"

(http://pages.ebay.com/help/account/search-tags.html).

Step 3: Build Links to Stores and Listings

To improve the search-engine ranking of your eBay Store, create as many links to your eBay Store as possible. Encourage your business partners to link to your eBay Store. Enter your Store into online directories such as Listmystore.com. Do not ignore the potential of links within eBay to boost your ranking - always link to your eBay Store from your listings and also from all of your guides or reviews.

Step 4: Track Your Performance

Once your have optimized your eBay presence, it is important to constantly track your performance and make improvements. All eBay Store sellers have access to traffic reports that allow you to see the keywords used to find your listings and the search engines that driving traffic to your Store (http://pages.ebay.com/help/specialtysites/traffic-reporting-basics.html). If you wish to see more in depth statistics, use Sellathon (http://www.sellathon.com), which can give you the traffic data for individual listings and pages.

Chapter 6:
Why Ebay auction fails?

EBay is one of the most popular auction web sites across the vastness of the internet. Many people make full-fledged businesses out of eBay auctions. Just as with any business, perhaps more so than other businesses, an eBay business can quickly and easily become a failure. There are a few sure-fire methods that will ensure that your eBay business becomes an almost instant failure. The following is our top seven reasons why eBay auctions fail.

Price

Price plays a big part in the success or failure of your eBay auction. If you set your starting price too high, bidders will look elsewhere. Many successful auctions set their prices low to begin with and leave it to the bidders to raise it higher. The same holds true for buy it now items (fixed price). If the price is too high, it will not sell, period. Aim a little lower for both. This area also includes shipping prices. If you charge excessively for shipping, it will keep bidders away.

Photograph

If you don't have a picture of your item, your customers will again look elsewhere. Bidders want to buy what they can see. If you provide at least one clear photograph of your item, it is more likely to sell then without any photographs at all.

Reserve Price

These are horrible words to a bidder. Bidders ant to bid freely and not worry about a reserve price. If you have something you want to minimum price for, you should consider a fixed price auction.

The Listing

If your listing is loud and flashy with an abundance of spelling errors or simply written in a way that no human being on earth could read it, your auction will fail. Ensure that all titles and text of the description are clear, concise, and clean.

Negative feedback

If you have negative feedback, you will have problems selling on eBay. Bidders want a seller they can trust.

PayPal

If you do not accept PayPal on eBay, you most likely fail. Most bidders on eBay use PayPal and ONLY PayPal. Consider creating an account for eBay purposes.

Being Difficult

You will want to avoid making statements in the listing that will make you appear as a difficult seller. You will want to be clear on your return policy, but do not be so strict in the policy or who you will sell to, that you put the bidder off your auctions forever. Be firm, but fair.

Chapter 7:
Some Auction Tips..!!

1. Managing your auction
The job is not over once the listing is posted. When your listing is "Live" on eBay the world is now part of your retail store. Customers will come in and out and look at your merchandise 24 hours a day.

Some of these customers will want to ask questions. They will usually do this via the eBay email messaging system. These eBay emails will be forwarded to your registered eMail account.

Email Security Note
It is very important for your security and that of your customers to never respond to a eBay member question via your registered email account. Always go to your "My eBay" control panel and select "messages" to read and respond to customer messages. eBay tries very hard to

reduce the fake or phishing scam emails but the task is nearly impossible. Some emails will look very official in your registered email account inbox but unless those messages are also within the eBay messaging system, they are not real and to answer one is a mistake. - Never sign in to eBay from any email sent to your account!

2. Once your listing is posted online the fun is just beginning. Some potential buyers will ask you questions about the item, and it's good practice to reply as quickly as possible. You might want to add to your listing if you think your answer would be useful to other buyers. Doing this also indicates to other bidders that you respond in a prompt and professional manner.

3. You can keep track on your item's progress using the "My eBay" tab at the top of the eBay homepage. Use this function to see how many bids you've received, the price you've achieved and how many peopleare watching your item.
Quick Tip - If your item has a great deal of "watchers" and you have a reserve price or Buy it Now price on the item, consider lowering these prices by a small amount about 24 hours before the end of the auction. eBay will notify each watcher of your item via eMail that you have

lowered the price. Your price only needs to be lowered by a small amount to get a free promotional email delivered directly to your prospective buyers!

4. As an anxious first-time seller, it can be disconcerting not to receive any bids in the first few days of the auction. You might be worried that you made a mistake when listing the item. Do not despair - eBay is becoming more advanced each day and so are eBay buyers. The seasoned buyers know to wait before bidding because they do not want to drive up the price or show their hand.

Inexperienced bidders will bid immediately but savvy eBay buyer waits till the last minute or uses a "sniping" program to buy your item in the last seconds of the auction. This invariably creates a "last minute flurry" of activity and your item may surge in price from $50.00 to $5000.00 in a matter of 10 seconds. Keep your cool, only lower that price once to get your emails out to the "watchers" and hold firm. You can't cancel or change the item with the last 12 hours in any case.

Quick Tip - When building your auction, make sure to include a "counter" so that you can see how many people are stopping by: it's a free option in the "Sell your item" form.

5. Safety for sellers

Some sellers will go into great detail within their listings telling buyers all of the forms of payment they will not take. This is done on the chance that a payment is fake or fraudulent. This is of course a concern but it is a concern of any business and is considered a cost of doing business in most retail circles. Protect yourself from these fraudulent payments by clearly stating your policy to not ship the item until the payment clears your banking institution. Use any length of time you wish to estimate the delay of shipment resulting from a less than stellar form of payment. Then offer quick shipping if the buyer uses your most secure and preferred form of payment.

6. Timing

When you're selling on eBay you choose the duration of your listing. Generally it's advisable to use seven-day or 10-day listings (additional fee) to get the most exposure, but if you're selling something like a concert ticket, or if you have items which are in high demand, like Wii Games or Hannah Montana collectibles a shorter listing would be best. (Turning inventory is preferable to long exposure).

If you start a seven-day listing, it ends exactly seven days later: make sure that your listing ends at an hour which will allow your item its best chance of selling (these hours of the day change depending upon the item, the best way to learn the best times to end an auction on any item is to use Terapeak research tools). Many sellers swear by ending their listings on Thursday and Sunday evenings when eBay is busiest.

7. Packaging

Take the utmost care when packaging your items for shipment. The U.S.P.S. has many resources available to help you learn how to ship if you are not set up already, (they even provide free boxes). Whatever method you use to ship, be sure your items are packed well and insured with some form of tracking capability.

Quick Tip - Use your business card as a return label on the outside of the box and throw some inside the box - Your buyer may remember you and you can get direct off eBay sales this way!

8. Follow Up

Always save your feedback as a seller. This is a policy which will save your feedback rating for when you need it most. Follow up with your buyers about 10 days after your shipment to be sure everything went well and to ask for positive feedback. If there was a problem, resolve it quickly and with little friction. But if you do receive negative feedback do not panic. You can always ask the buyer to mutually remove negative feedback if you have saved yours for this purpose. Some buyers will leave a negative by mistake or because they had a bad day. These buyers do not want a negative on their account any more than you do... It's a tough world out there; sometimes we have to see it through business-like eyes. Your feedback is your business reputation on eBay and you should protect it with all of your capable efforts to do so. If you did not deserve a negative rating you have every right to try an get the buyer to remove it.

9. Set up a System

OK, now you have gotten your feet wet on eBay - What's next?

Set up a repeatable system of selling. You need to find ways to reduce the time wasted making listings and re-listing of items. There are numerous software suites available to help your company do this. Some are free, and some are costly. The features you will require will vary with your business plan. Staffing, inventory, and goals... But once you have a listing software suite installed, your eBay business will become a well oiled machine for marketing your products to the world.

Chapter 8:
12 Items You CAN'T Sell On EBay

1. Knock offs of music, TV shows or movies. The "bootleg" movies, for example, are often made by guys who sneak a movie camera into a newly-released movie where presumably, they crouch behind a seat and make a crummy copy. There is a large production of these counterfeit items in Asia where US laws have no power.

2. Software and computer games can likewise be copied and their sale is illegal by all US laws. Naturally, the items above may be sold if you have a copy that you purchased legitimately and no longer want.

3. The so-called "replica" market for handbags, designer sunglasses and clothing is definitely forbidden although these items are often sold in physical stores around the US. Ironically, when attending eBay Live In New Orleans in 2004, we found a store in one of their famous markets selling replica purses that were not allowed on eBay.

4. Lazy and less-than-honest sellers often steal copyrighted material from other sellers. This has happened to me many times and eBay has a program called VERO (Verified Rights Owner) that will remove offending auctions, although there seems to be no penalty attached to the seller, which is unfortunate.

5. Alcoholic beverage sales are not allowed although a beverage "container', especially those of wine, may be sold for its value.

6. Cigarettes, cigars, smokeless tobacco or coupons for such items are not permitted on eBay.com.
The eBay rules for collectible tobacco and

alcohol containers are the same:
* The value of the item is in the collectible packaging, not in the wine/tobacco itself.
* The listing description should state that the package has not been opened, but that the twine/tobacco within is not for consumption.
* The collectible tobacco packaging must not be available at any retail outlet, and packaging must have a value that substantially exceeds the current retail price of that wine/tobacco product in the package.
* Sellers must take steps to ensure that the buyer of these collectibles is at least 18 years of age

7. Firearms are strictly regulated by US law and may not be sold on eBay.

8. Satellite and cable TV descramblers are forbidden by the Federal Trade Commission.

9. Animals and wildlife products may not be sold, which includes stuffed birds and pelts from endangered species. There are limited sales of ivory, tortoise shell, marine products and other items relating to animals. This area is quite complex and any would-be seller needs to

thoroughly understand the various laws before getting involved in these sales.

10. Event tickets have state-by-state laws that make their sale complex. Some states, for instance, forbid anyone to make more than a few dollars in profit (or no profit at all) on the resale of tickets.

11. Listing a catalog of items that a seller offers for sale is forbidden. The only catalogs legally sold on eBay are collectible kinds, such as an old Sears Roebuck or Montgomery Wards catalog that is memorabilia and doesn't offer current merchandise for sale.

12. Raffles and prizes are 100% prohibited. According to eBay, such promotions are highly regulated and may be unlawful in many states.
There are other kinds of merchandise that a seller may not sell on eBay, so carefully check eBay rules before listing anything. It's much better to know the rules in advance of spending money that can't be recouped.

ALL RIGHTS RESERVED. No part of this publication may be reproduced or transmitted in any form whatsoever, electronic, or mechanical, including photocopying, recording, or by any informational storage or retrieval system without express written, dated and signed permission from the author.

DISCLAIMER AND/OR LEGAL NOTICES: Every effort has been made to accurately represent this book and it's potential. Results vary with every individual, and your results may or may not be different from those depicted. No promises, guarantees or warranties, whether stated or implied, have been made that you will produce any specific result from this book. Your efforts are individual and unique, and may vary from those shown. Your success depends on your efforts, background and motivation.

The material in this publication is provided for educational and informational purposes only. Use of the programs, advice, and information contained in this book is at the sole choice and risk of the reader.

Printed in Great Britain
by Amazon.co.uk, Ltd.,
Marston Gate.